WONDERS
OF THE LAND

Written by
Osman Kaplan

Illustrated by
Öznur Kalender

12 11 10 09   1 2 3 4

Published by Tughra Books
26 Worlds Fair Dr. Unit C,
Somerset, NJ, 08873, USA
www.tughrabooks.com

Wonders of the Land

Written by Osman Kaplan
Illustrated by Öznur Kalender

ISBN: 978-1-59784-145-0

Printed by Çağlayan A.Ş. Izmir, Turkey

CONTENTS

The Spider that Can Use a Lasso

Hurray! Look how slippery my thread is! My home is strong too. I built my home with my strong, elastic threads, and I constructed my elevator with my slippery threads. My elevator is not like yours. It is just the way I wanted it. It is made of a thread that I hang down my home. For a creature like me that has a home made of thread, it is not really surprising to have a thread elevator, is it?

My Lord designed my body in such a way that I can do this. The chemicals that are used in

the human body to form finger-
nails and toenails are used in my
body to make thread. I can do
whatever I want with this thread.

We have a special kind of thread
for each purpose. All of them are
designed to meet our needs. The
ones that we use to build our

Do you know that the sticky fibers we make are the best to catch our prey? Especially for my species, Bolas spiders. We use a lasso to catch our prey. Our favorite prey is that moth, the little bug which eats your woolen clothes.

The first thing I do before we go moth hunting is to prepare my sticky thread. Then I start spreading a special smell. Actually, this is just an imitation of a smell that moths use to communicate. Any moth, which catches the scent, thinks that another moth is calling. When it is trying to reach where the smell is coming from, it does not realize how close it is getting to me. Then I use my sticky thread as a lasso and catch it. Thanks be to our Lord for teaching us how to imitate that smell! Otherwise, we would not be able to catch our prey since we cannot leave our homes.

houses are strong and flexible; the ones for elevator construction are slippery; and the ones that we use for hunting are sticky.

I eat some of the moths right after I catch them. I carefully wrap up in my thread the ones that I want to eat later. This means I can store my food until I unpack it again later when I am hungry.

IDENTITY CARD

We live in warm areas. Unlike most of our relatives we do not weave a web and wait for a bug or a fly to get entangled in it. Instead, we spread a smell that attracts moths, and then we catch the moths that are attracted to our smell with the lasso we make.

The Expert at Running Away

With this exit I am about to finish building, my den will have three exits. It is really important for us foxes to have more than one exit for our safety. Sometimes hunters follow us with their dogs and we need to take refuge in our dens. We urinate in front of our den just before we enter it. The hunters who are following us realize that we have just entered the den. They think that we are still inside, and they keep waiting for us to come out again, but they are waiting for nothing because we have already escaped by the safest exit while they are waiting outside!

A few days ago, hunters were following one of my friends. As my friend was running out of the back exit of the den, one of the dogs saw him and started following him. Of course, the other dogs started chasing him too. The dogs found him easy to track since he was leaving his scent behind him. So he jumped into a river to hide his trail because dogs cannot smell us anymore if we dive into water. The dogs waited and looked for him stubbornly. But they could not tell where my friend had gone. In the end, they gave up and went back, so my friend had managed to get rid of them.

We feel lucky if we come to a river when hunters are chasing us. But what if we do not see a river? If our home is far away or if there is no river close by, we have to find another way. For example, we sometimes step on

cattle dung on purpose. This way we smell like cattle. Since dogs hate that smell, they stop follow-

ing us. Thanks be to God Almighty, we know how to act in every event! Think about it. If we had not been taught all these tricks, we might have become extinct by now!

IDENTITY CARD

I am about 2 feet tall; however, if you include my tail, I can be as tall as 3 feet. We foxes can live in almost any part of the world. Our color may vary according to the region we live. I have relatives whose colors are white, red, brown, or sand. My nose is long, my ears are upright, and my eyes are round. I weigh around 15 pounds.

Fungus Farmers

I will be done if I just take this last leaf lying on the ground. I have cut a lot of leaves today, and I am tired now. After having a rest, I will chew the leaves that I have collected because I need these cut leaves to get my nourishment. By the way, I do not chew the leaves to eat them. Even if I did eat them, it would not do me any good. In fact it would be harmful because I am a leaf ant and my stomach is not created in a way that it can digest plants.

So, my friends and I use leaves for another purpose. Do you know what for?

First of all, we cut the leaves using our jawbones. Then we carry the leaves on top of our heads to our home. We chew the leaves that we have stacked earlier in our home to make a big pile. Then we lay these leaf piles on the ground to grow fungus on them. The buds that grow on fungi are our food.

However, we have to store them carefully. You store your food in the refrigerator, right? We do similar things to prevent our leaves getting spoilt. We adjust the temperature and humidity of the room where we keep our leaf stacks. I always thank God Almighty for teaching us all these things before we were even born. Otherwise, we would not know how to find food, and we would have been dead pretty soon after we were born!

We are safe when we are working in our home. However we are not very safe in the outside world. The most dangerous thing is to meet a fly while we are carrying a leaf. When we are carrying leaves, flies can harm us.

So we bring some of our friends to protect us from the flies. These friends are usually smaller members of our family. On our way home, we carry them on top of the leaves. In case of an attack, our small friends protect us from above. We can live safely because we help each other like this.

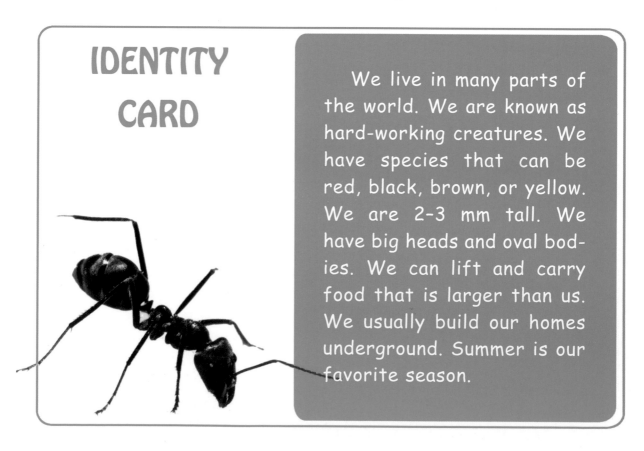

IDENTITY CARD

We live in many parts of the world. We are known as hard-working creatures. We have species that can be red, black, brown, or yellow. We are 2–3 mm tall. We have big heads and oval bodies. We can lift and carry food that is larger than us. We usually build our homes underground. Summer is our favorite season.

Little Architects

It is fortunate that we constructed this nice ventilation system. Otherwise, I think we would have fainted or died in this hot weather. My! It is really hot today. We termites live in places where the climate is hot. Sometimes it rains suddenly and heavily. So we build a roof on our homes to protect them from the rain. I am sure you want to know more about our homes. So I, a guard termite, am going to tell you some more about them.

Our homes, which are narrow at the front and wide at the sides, can be as tall as 20 feet. The narrow sides face north and south, while the wider sides face east and west. The reason why we build our homes that way is to protect ourselves from too much

wind and sunlight. There are other precautions that we take inside our homes to avoid wind and sunlight. For instance, we have a perfect ventilation system throughout our building, which has several floors. If our homes are still hot in spite of the ventilation, we wet the walls with our special saliva to cool them down.

Our buildings look like your skyscrapers, and in the middle our queen has her own room. The rooms that surround this main room are reserved for eggs and baby termites. Then, teenage and adult termites are in the next rooms that surround the egg and baby rooms. The outermost rooms are for our soldier friends and for growing fungus.

You might be saying, "Good job termites! How well organized your homes are! You have even made a roof for your homes to shelter from the rain. What is more, you manage to do all this hard work despite your small bodies."

Then I must tell you one more thing that is even more surprising. Do you know that we cannot see? Yes, we are blind, and we do all these things that I have been telling you about without seeing a thing!

Actually, you could say our home is more like a city than a skyscraper because our ventilation, heating, and air-conditioning systems work perfectly. Moreover, in our city every termite, including the queen and the older termites, has a task of its own to carry out. The soldier termites protect our city. Perfect cooperation can be seen everywhere.

Our queen rules our city fairly. We all do our duties and we are all happy and satisfied. We will continue to inspire you with our construction systems that were taught to us by God Almighty.

IDENTITY CARD

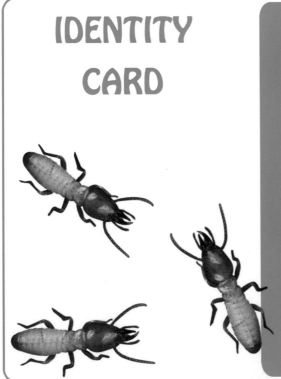

We termites are considered skyscraper construction experts. We build our homes in regions where there is no winter. God Almighty taught us how to construct our homes, which are similar to human beings' skyscrapers, even though we are blind. We have a perfect organization and task assignment system. Both old and young termites do their duties perfectly.

Weight Lifter

A couple of days ago, a farmer who was working above cut off my tail with his pickaxe. Of course, my farmer friend was not aware of what he had done. He was just trying to dig over the ground so that he could plant some seeds. Having my tail cut off does not really bother me anyway. It will grow back to its normal size soon because I am a worm. My body consists of many rings. Losing a few of them does not mean that I am going to die.

Our Exalted Lord, God Almighty, created us so we are able to grow back our lost body parts, even our head. What a great feature to have, right? Can

21

you imagine our lives without this ability? We would die easily because our homes are under the ground. My experience with my farmer friend is something common that can happen to us at any time.

Our presence under the ground is important for human beings as well. We are always building tunnels and opening new roads under the ground. In this way, we mix and loosen the soil. At the same time, we also carry the fertile soil layer to the top. So, the soil becomes more fertile.

Our body weight is only a couple of grams, but in spite of our light weight, we can move soil layers that are sixty times heavier than we are. That is like a human carrying tons of stuff. So that we can succeed in this difficult duty, our body is covered with muscles. We first shrink the front part of our body to make it thin by tightening these muscles. We then push our head into a small hole in the layer of soil. Then, we use our muscles again to make our body fatter. In this way we make the hole in the soil layer bigger. We keep wriggling through the soil by repeating these tightening and expanding actions.

If we cannot find a hole to push our head into or we come up against something hard, we follow another plan. First, we spit on the target surface. Once our saliva has made it softer, we take a bite out of it. In this way, we eat all the rotten plant and animal leftovers stored inside the soil.

It is fortunate that we are here, always working to freshen up the soil and eating the remains left in it. Otherwise, the soil would become hard and infertile in a short time. Then, farmers would not be able to grow lots of good food, and human life would be affected in a very bad way.

IDENTITY CARD

We live under the ground. We are about 9 inches long and we weigh just a few grams. We worms are responsible for increasing the fertility of the soil. You can see us in red, yellow, and brown colors. We obtain our food from soil by eating animal and plant remains.

Stinky Stuff

That puma approaching me is most probably considering me for his dinner. I should get closer to make him recognize me. I guess he has not seen that I am a skunk. Otherwise, he would have run away. I do not want to use my smelly stuff right away. First I should let him know who I am. Yes, he has finally seen me clearly. Since he knows what is waiting for him, he is running away. If he had tried attacking, I would have had to defend myself.

We skunks do not need to hide from our enemies because

God Almighty gave us a very good way of defending ourselves. Whenever we face any danger, we spray an oily liquid from our body into our enemy's face to protect ourselves. The smell of the liquid is unbearable, and it lasts for a long time. You cannot get rid of that smell easily. The stinky liquid may even burn the skin that it touches. If it hits an attacker's eyes, he can go blind for a while.

For this reason, we first warn our enemies. Most times our warning works; however, sometimes our attacker does not realize that we are about to spray our terrible smell. The attacker just keeps coming towards us. Then we do not have any choice left but to use our smelly spray.

In my body, I store enough smelly liquid to spray as many as six times. If I run low, I produce more of it. My body is created in such a way as to produce more of this liquid as I need it. Humans copy this feature of ours. They have studied the chemistry of our smell. Now they can produce perfumes that last longer than the ones they had before.

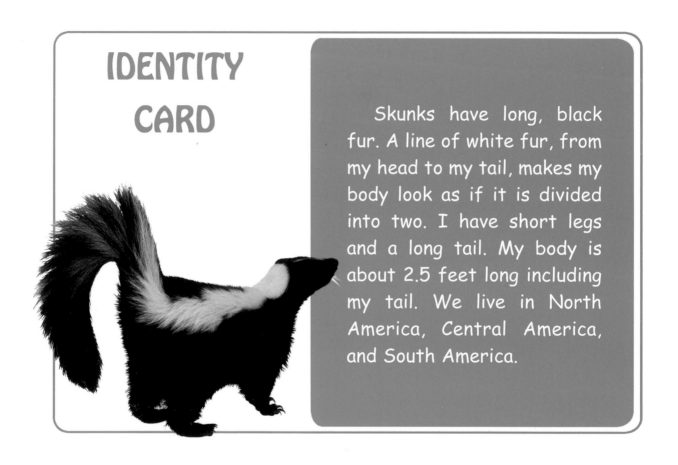

IDENTITY CARD

Skunks have long, black fur. A line of white fur, from my head to my tail, makes my body look as if it is divided into two. I have short legs and a long tail. My body is about 2.5 feet long including my tail. We live in North America, Central America, and South America.

Tunnel Experts

My friends and I have been digging since this morning. We are so tired, but we have almost completed the tunnel. We will be done after removing this pile of soil. I have to tell my friend to lie on his back again so that we can load the soil on top of his belly.

Then we can drag him outside by pulling his legs. Our tunnel will be clean after this last step.

If you are wondering what kind of creatures we are that move soil by using our friend as a cart, let me tell you. We are tunnel experts—badgers. These

tunnels that we have carved under the ground are our homes. Our Lord, God Almighty, created our claws hard and strong so that we can use them for digging. He also taught us everything that we need to know to open up tunnels. Otherwise we would not be able to figure out how to carry this spare soil out of the tunnel.

The first thing we do is to choose the best soil to make our burrow in because not every type of soil is suitable for tunnels. If we do not find a good place for our burrow, it might collapse and we could all die. The ideal type of soil is usually composed mostly of sand.

After finding the perfect soil type, we start digging. Of course, we follow a plan. We do not start digging just anyhow. We make several floors, and we make sure that there is at least one exit at the end of each floor. It is important that the exits face south, because exits that open to the north can get flooded and let in the cold wind.

The tunnel that we completed today also opens to the south. While I have been talking about us, we have carried the remaining soil out of the tunnel. We are already done.

IDENTITY CARD

Our legs are short but strong. We use our claws to build tunnels. Our average weight is around 44 pounds and we are 3 feet tall. Our nose can detect smells very well. Our color may be gray, black, or lead. We badgers mostly live in Europe and Asia.

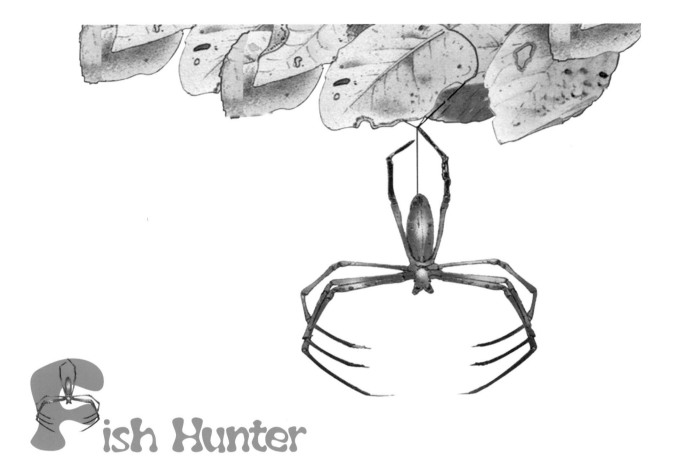

Fish Hunter

I was almost the victim then, when I was trying to catch my prey. The weight of the fish I caught almost toppled me into the water. He is a fish and I am a spider, and so he is heavier than me, of course.

Fortunately, I realized pretty quickly that the dead fish was pulling me down into the river. I turned upside down on the water to carry him on my belly. Then I lifted him up and pulled him to the side.

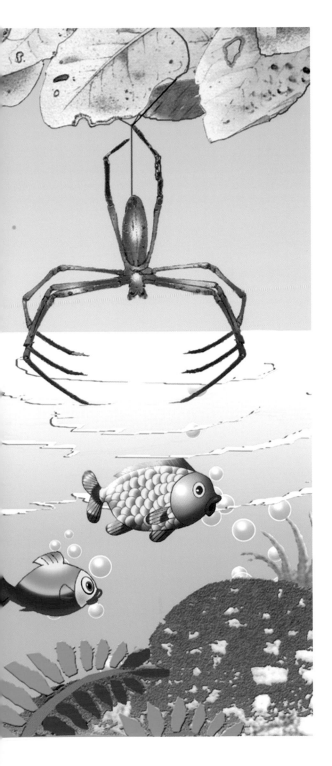

By the way, it was not hard for me to lift him because I used the force of the water. The water raised the fish and made it lighter for me. Now it is time to eat my catch. Let me tell you about how I hunt my prey from the beginning.

We Dolomedes spiders spend most of our time fishing in rivers. We use our legs as a fishing line. First, I dip four of my legs into the river and use my other four legs to hold on to land. My four legs dipped in the water do not sink because I lick them first. In this way, I cover them with a special waterproof liquid produced in my mouth.

Next, I wait for a fish to get close. First, I catch it with my legs that are in the water. Then I put it in my mouth and poison it with another special liquid that is hidden in my teeth. When the poison starts working on the fish, it becomes ready to be swallowed and digested easily. That is how we spiders can eat fish easily. Of course, the poison, which works on the fish, does not do us any harm. Actually it is a gift from God Almighty for our benefit.

While I have been telling you my story, the fish has become ready to eat. I am so hungry. I shall start eating now.

IDENTITY CARD

We live among the plants growing around the river. We are $\frac{3}{4}$ inches tall. We live in countries with a warm climate. Unlike our other spider friends, we do not choose easy targets. Even though we live on land, we like fishing. God Almighty gave us special features to be able to catch fish.

The Best Jumpers

If I jump three or four more times, I might catch up with that cat. Then, I can settle on him. Thanks be to God Almighty, I can jump. Otherwise, I would most probably be starving, for I get the nourishment I need from the animals I live on. If I were not able to jump, I would not be able to move from one place to another. If you think carefully about it, a tiny flea like me would first need to get off one animal, and then walk to the next ani-

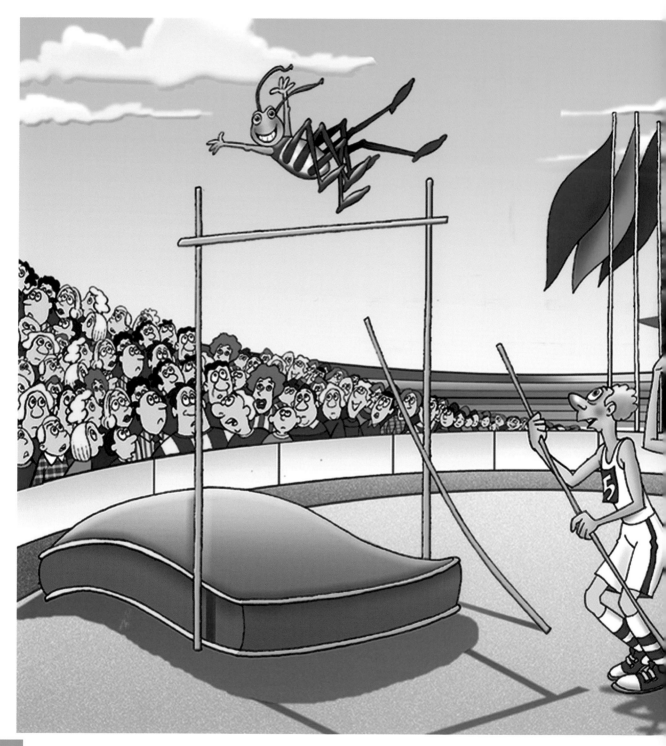

mal. It might take me many hours to cover even a one-foot distance.

We fleas are only $1/8$ inches long, but if we use all our power we can jump as high as two hundred times our length. That makes eighteen inches up and one foot forward each jump. If humans were created to jump like us, they would go up as high as 600 feet and go forward as far as 820 feet.

You may think that our legs are extremely strong. In fact, our leg muscles are not strong enough to be able to jump that far. We have another feature that helps us to do that. God Almighty has granted us spring-like legs. When we want to jump, we kneel down and stretch out this spring system. That causes a stress on our legs. Then we jump up as a result of that stress. The structure of our legs is more complicated and elastic than any material human beings have ever made.

Every rise ends with a fall. When I am jumping, I go higher and higher, and then I fall downwards onto my back or head, but that fall does not do me any harm. God Almighty has created my body very soft and elastic. My skin is not as hard as the skin of other bugs. My heart works very slowly so quick rises and falls do not affect it. In other words, I do not have to worry about getting injured when I hit the ground. I can jump as much as I want!

IDENTITY CARD

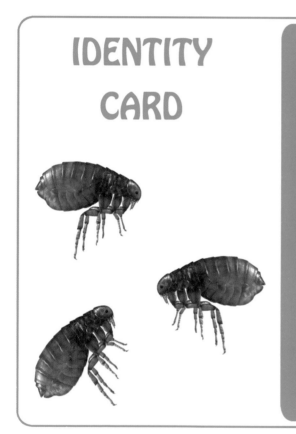

We fleas are really tiny. We mostly live on dogs and cats. Our greatest ability is being able to jump two hundred times higher than our own size. God Almighty has created our body elastic enough to protect us from being injured when we come back down. So we are not injured even if we hit the ground on our head.

 Colorful Life

It took several hours for me to climb this tree, but it is sure going to be worth it. I cannot find so many insects and flies anywhere else. However, I should hide myself carefully. Otherwise, they will see me and try to escape.

Then all my effort climbing up here will be in vain. I should change my skin color to match the color of the branch I am sitting on. I think you understand that I am a chameleon when I tell you that I can change my color.

We chameleons can adapt to the color of our environment in about fifteen minutes. If we could not do that, life would be really difficult for us. Birds of prey could spot us quickly and catch us, for we move very slowly compared to them. There is no way that we could run away from them. When we imitate the color of the environment around us, neither the hunters who are after us, nor our prey can see us.

God Almighty created our eyes different than the eyes of other animals, and our skin is different too. Each of our eyes can work separately at the same time. In this way, we can watch a fly passing by with one eye while we are on the alert for our enemies with the other.

We can trap our prey quickly in one step. Let me tell you how we do it, if you are curious about how we, such slow-moving animals, can catch flying insects. Being slow does not stop us from hunting. We do not move when we are hunting anyway. We trap flies with our tongue. Our tongue is almost as long as our body length, and it is long and sticky at the end. Also, the end of our tongue is like a mace. First, I hit my prey with this mace to weaken it. Then, I catch it with the sticky side of my tongue and pull it in. Our Creator taught us how to carry our long tongue as well as use it. When we are done with hunting, we roll up our tongue neatly and keep it in our mouth.

Yes, as I guessed, there are swarms of flies here. I had better catch a few before they get away.

IDENTITY CARD

We chameleons live mainly in Africa and Madagascar, but some of us live in southern Europe and Asia. We are slow-moving animals. For hunting, we use our tongues, which we roll up and keep in our mouths otherwise. Our tongue is as long as our body. Our most distinctive feature is the ability to change our color according to our surroundings. In this way, we can hide ourselves both from our prey and from creatures that are hunting us.

Desert Vehicle

We have been walking for almost an hour. We have a long way to travel through the desert. My owner made a good decision by choosing me as a vehicle. What kind of animal other than the camel can endure the harsh conditions of the desert?

The biggest danger in the desert is drought. Guess what? We are good at dealing with it. We can drink as much as one third of our weight in water at once. Then we can live for three to four weeks without drinking again. Since my owner knows

me, he let me drink a lot of water this morning. As I walk, my body burns the fat stored in my humps to give me energy. This fat-burning also produces water in my body. So, both my need for water and energy are provided at the same time.

pounds of hay every day for a month and still be fine. We camels are not picky when it comes to food anyway. If we have a break here, I can eat these cactuses and bushes. My lips, tongue and stomach were created in a way to be protected from thorns.

Do you know what I have figured out? When my owner gets off me, it is really hard for him to walk on sand. His feet sink into sand. As for me, I do not have any problem like that, for God Almighty created the bottom of my feet so wide that I can walk on sand very easily. He also created the bottom of my feet with a thick layer of skin so that I do not feel the heat at all, as I walk on the burning hot desert sand.

The first day of our journey will be over as soon as the sun sets. I hope the rest of our journey will be as easy as today so we can arrive our destination

It is also hard to find food in the desert. My owner has brought some food for me to eat on our journey. We can eat as little as 4

quickly. If there is a sand storm, our journey will take longer. But actually, our All-Merciful God has helped us to overcome that problem too. He has given us long, thick eyelashes in order to protect our eyes from sand particles. We also have muscles in our nose that we can use to close our nostrils to prevent sand getting into our noses. We are slowing down. That means we are about to stop. That is good because I am tired.

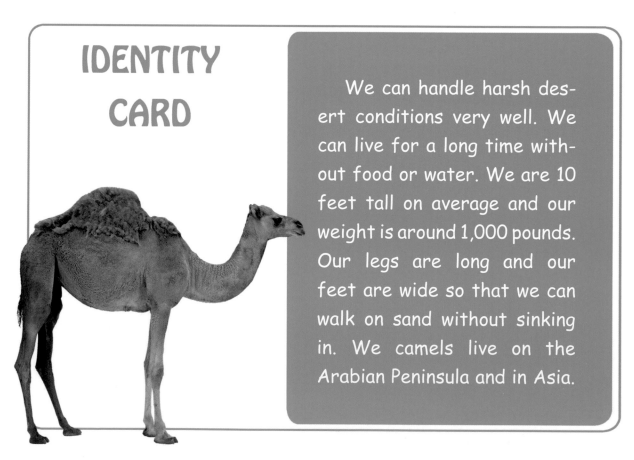

IDENTITY CARD

We can handle harsh desert conditions very well. We can live for a long time without food or water. We are 10 feet tall on average and our weight is around 1,000 pounds. Our legs are long and our feet are wide so that we can walk on sand without sinking in. We camels live on the Arabian Peninsula and in Asia.

Weather Forecast Experts

I guess we will need to go back home early today. It is getting more humid. It looks like it will rain soon. Now we should keep our tails between our legs. That way, our goatherd can see that it's going to rain and we will be able to get back to his home before it starts raining.

Unlike us, humans cannot tell if it's going to rain, so we have to use our sign language to let them know. Then, the goatherd gathers our flock to take us to shelter quickly.

We are not the only animals that can forecast the weather and give signs about it. God Almighty has given this ability to our other friends too. For instance, if horses get bad-tempered and mice block the entrances to their nest with grass that means it is going to rain that day. To name a couple more—donkeys grouping together and crows being noisy are other signs of rain.

If the birds start singing early in the morning, the weather will be bright and sunny. Our bird friends usually quit singing when it gets warmer around noontime. If it is going to be warm again the next day, they start singing again in the afternoon. Swallows, moles, and spiders are our other friends that can inform us about the weather. If the weather will be fine, swallows fly higher than normal, moles build their tunnels, and spiders weave their webs.

The behavior of some of our friends can even give clues about all seasons. For example, if deer

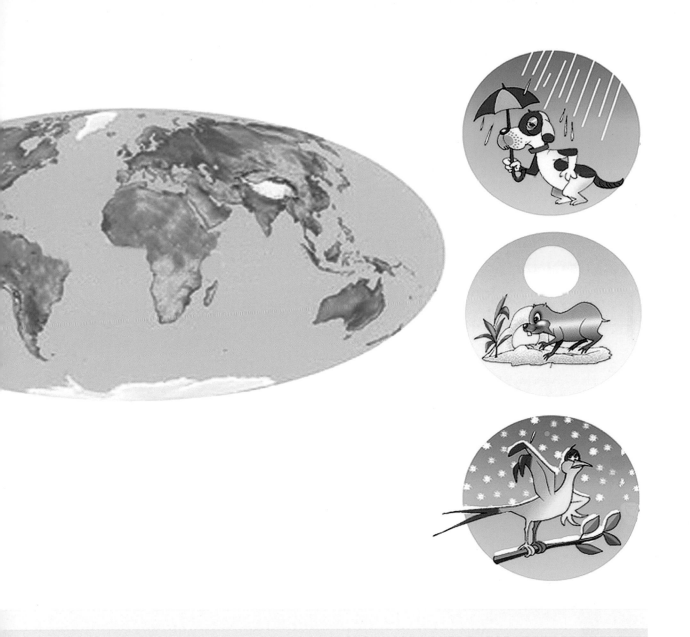

are searching hard for food, that means it will be a harsh winter. If spiders are aggressive in autumn, the cold winter weather is going to start soon. Some of our friends give messages about the coming summer. For example, turtles lay their eggs deeper in the sand, if it will be a hot and humid summer.

Being aware of the weather conditions helps us and our other animal friends. It means we can take precautions to protect ourselves from too much heat or cold. Of course, that helps our human friends too. They can get an idea of how the weather is going to be by simply watching us.

Yes, we were right again. It has started raining already and we have arrived at the farm just in time. Our tail signals saved our goatherd and us from getting wet!

IDENTITY CARD

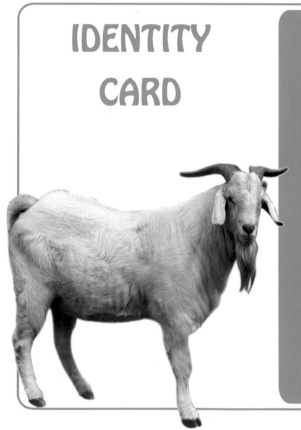

We live with humans and eat grass and bushes. We like the buds on trees. Our relatives live free in the mountains. They are bigger and faster compared to us. They can even climb up sharp rocks and cliff. Our length and weight can vary according to our species. Our hair is long. We goats live almost in any part of the world.

Communication Experts

Today we had a family trip to the woods. When we were walking around, I held on to my mom's tail with my trunk as usual because I did not want to get lost. My mom takes care of me very well, and she protects me from all kinds of dangers. When I am with my mom, even a tiger cannot find the courage to hurt me.

Of course, you must have realized that I am a baby elephant when you read the beginning of my story. For now I am small, but when I get older I will be extremely big. My mom said that we elephants are the biggest animals on land. Our giant bodies are almost as big as a truck. Our ears and teeth are also big like our trunk.

My trunk that I use to hold my mom's tail is actually my nose. However, we use our trunks for almost everything. The best use of our trunk is when my mom pets me with hers.

My big ears are as useful as my trunk. I should mention that my ears are extremely sensitive. I can hear noises coming from very far away. My mom says, "Thanks be to God Almighty that our ears were created very sensitive." I guess she is right. Otherwise, how would I communicate with my friends who live far away? Sometimes I sense danger and I want to warn my friends. Then I strike the ground with my feet. The vibrations from my stamping can be heard by my friends. So they understand what I am trying to say.

Did you know that I use my ears not only for hearing but also for speaking? Don't tell me that I cannot talk with my ears. Actually, it is another way of communication. It is like a sign language. When I want to talk to my friends, I move my ears to express myself.

Sometimes it gets too hot and I use my ears like a fan. I get cool as I wave them back and forth.

As I am getting older I realize that God created every organ I have so as to make my life easier. I mean, with the features that I have now, I can good take care of myself. However, I still live with my parents like other elephants do because we have a very organized and disciplined social life. I always show respect to elderly members of my family. We support each other whenever we are in need. I am sure that if I need any help, there will be someone to help me. Isn't that nice?

IDENTITY CARD

We are the biggest animals who live on land. We are 13 feet tall and we weigh around 5-6 tons. Our life span determined by God Almighty is around 50-60 years. Our ears look like huge hand fans. However, our trunk is more interesting than our ears because our trunk looks like a large, long hose. We do almost everything with our trunk. Most of us live in Africa and Asia.